THE BULLY-FREE ZONE

DON'T BE A BULLY!

THERESE HARASYMIW

PowerKiDS
press.

New York

Published in 2021 by The Rosen Publishing Group, Inc.
29 East 21st Street, New York, NY 10010

First Edition

Portions of this work were originally authored by Addy Ferguson and published as *Are You a Bully?* All new material this edition authored by Therese Harasymiw.

Editor: Therese Harasymiw
Book Design: Reann Nye

Photo Credits: Cover kali9/iStock /Getty Images Plus/Getty Images; series art Here/Shutterstock.com; p. 5 Rido/Shutterstock.com; p. 7 Africa Studio/Shutterstock.com; p. 9 SpeedKingz/Shutterstock.com; p. 11 DGLimages/Shutterstock.com; p. 13 stefanel/Shutterstock.com; p. 15 kali9/E+/Getty Images; p. 17 Viktoriia Hnatiuk/Shutterstock.com; p. 19 Pixel-Shot/Shutterstock.com; p. 21 Compassionate Eye Foundation/Steven Errico/DigitalVision/Getty Images; p. 22 Rebecca Nelson/DigitalVision/Getty Images.

Library of Congress Cataloging-in-Publication Data

Names: Harasymiw, Therese, author.
Title: Don't be a bully / Therese Harasymiw.
Description: New York : PowerKids Press, [2021] | Series: The bully-free
   zone | Includes index.
Identifiers: LCCN 2019056360 | ISBN 9781725319400 (paperback) | ISBN
   9781725319424 (library binding) | ISBN 9781725319417 (6 pack)
Subjects: LCSH: Bullying–Juvenile literature.
Classification: LCC BF637.B85 H354 2021 | DDC 302.34/3–dc23
LC record available at https://lccn.loc.gov/2019056360

Manufactured in the United States of America

Some of the images in this book illustrate individuals who are models. The depictions do not imply actual situations or events.

CPSIA Compliance Information: Batch #CSPK20. For Further Information contact Rosen Publishing, New York, New York at 1-800-237-9932.

Find us on

CONTENTS

TIME TO STOP

It's common for kids to tease each other. However, this behavior should stop once the person being teased says, "Stop." When a child continues to tease, **taunt**, or harm another child in some way, this is bullying. Bullies repeat unwanted **aggressive** behavior on purpose in order to hurt someone else.

If you think you might have bullied others, read this book. It will help you understand the kinds of bullying and why people who bully do it. Most important, you'll learn tips about how to stop bullying and help the people who have been hurt by it.

IN THE ZONE

The U.S. government website Stopbullying.gov explains more about bullying. Bullies use power, such as popularity or strength, to harm others. But not all bullies are popular or strong.

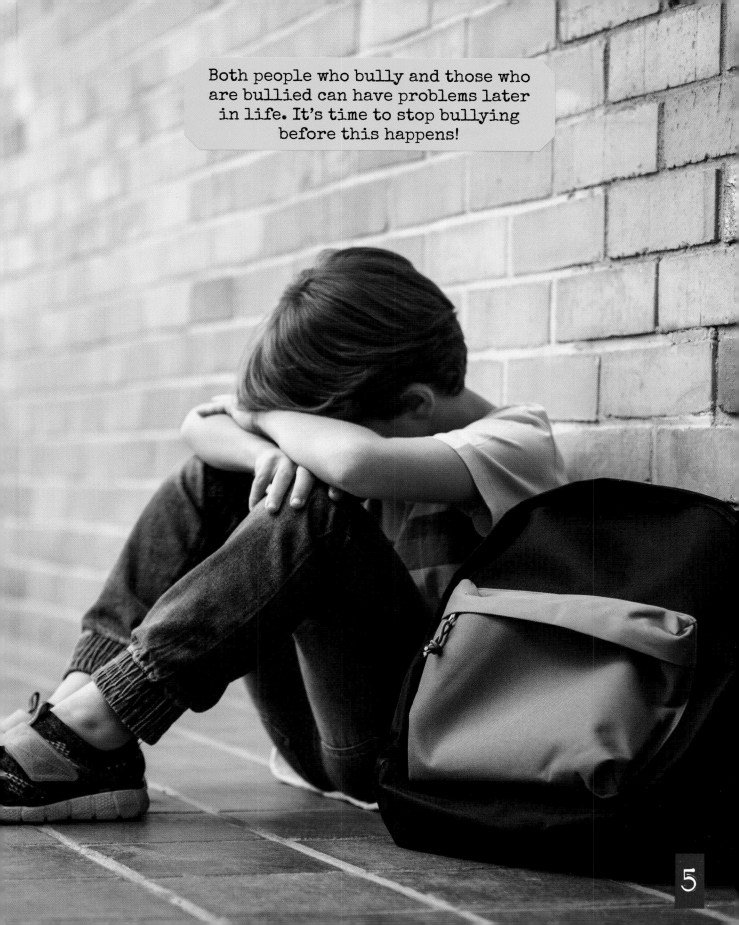

Both people who bully and those who are bullied can have problems later in life. It's time to stop bullying before this happens!

BULLYING BEHAVIORS

There are different kinds of bullies and different bullying behaviors. All are harmful. Some bullies hurt their victims by being physically aggressive, such as hitting or pushing. This might be what you think of as bullying, but there are more ways bullies can hurt others.

Some bullies use words to harm or scare. These are verbal bullies. Other bullies' behaviors are more hidden. They hurt others by trying to ruin their friendships. These social bullies may stop people from being a part of a group and try to get others to go along with them. Cyberbullies use email, **social networks**, and texts to attack people.

IN THE ZONE

Spreading **rumors** is a kind of social bullying. It's meant to harm someone's **reputation**.

Online bullying, or cyberbullying, is just as harmful as face-to-face bullying. Sometimes police are called to find out who a cyberbully is.

SOUND FAMILIAR?

Has anyone ever called you a bully? Think about what happened. Did you use some kind of power against someone? Did you act against someone with force or **threaten** to? Did you spread an **embarrassing** story about someone?

Bullies sometimes don't know they are bullying. They're used to treating others a certain way. It might not seem wrong to them because it's just the way they've always acted. Maybe they're trying to get other people's approval by being mean. Bullies may even think that others deserve the harm being done to them. It's still bullying, and it's still wrong.

It isn't always one person doing the bullying. Sometimes a group of bullies gangs up on someone.

SOME WAYS THAT PEOPLE BULLY

- Push or hit others
- Call others names
- Try to scare or upset others
- Spread rumors
- Tease others about how they look or act
- Ask other people to do mean things
- Leave people out of a group on purpose
- Take others' things
- Send mean messages by phone or computer

9

IN THE MIND OF THE BULLY

Even though it's always wrong to bully, people often do it for a reason. They may have learned to bully from someone else. Sometimes a person bullies others to feel better about themselves. Bullies may not have many friends or think they have to bully because their friends bully. Sometimes bullies are angry about something happening in their lives. Bullies may have someone bullying them too!

Whatever the reason, bullies can learn to act differently. It isn't easy, but it will make their life better as well as the life of the person they bully.

WHY STOP?

If you've recognized a bullying behavior as something you've done, know that you can and should stop today. Think about how it makes the other person feel. Trying to understand their feelings is called empathy. If you were in their place, you would want the bullying to end too.

The effects of bullying can be serious and long-lasting. Bullied kids feel lonely and scared. They often withdraw from activities and friendships. They might start doing poorly in school or even avoid going to school. Even more serious, some bullying victims hurt themselves to stop feeling the pain caused by bullying.

IN THE ZONE

Kids who are bullied are twice as likely as those who haven't been to have health issues such as headaches.

Victims of bullying may have low **self-esteem** and have a hard time feeling good about themselves even after the bullying stops.

CHANGING YOUR CHOICES

Bullying is a choice. Not bullying is another choice. You can start making this better choice. If you want—and choose—to stop bullying behaviors, there are people who can help you build new patterns of behavior.

First, talk to an adult you trust, such as a parent, teacher, or school **counselor**. Tell this person what you're thinking and feeling. Don't be embarrassed or worried about getting in trouble. If you make it clear that you're trying to change, people will want to help you. Together, you can make a plan for how to change bullying behaviors.

The first step to stop being a bully is deciding to stop!

TAKING RESPONSIBILITY

Taking responsibility for your bullying should be part of your plan to stop. Being able to tell yourself and others that what you did was wrong will help you change. Saying you're sorry, or apologizing, to the people you've bullied is an important way to take responsibility for your actions.

The person you bullied might not be willing to accept your apology at first. They may be angry with you, scared of you, or mistrust you. However, kind and supportive actions, such as sticking up for them, can show them that you really have changed.

IN THE ZONE

A study reported that more than half of all bullying situations stop when someone sticks up for the person being bullied.

People with empathy who realize that everyone deserves respect aren't likely to bully others.

17

YOU'RE IN CONTROL

Changing bullying ways can be hard work. Sometimes it means telling friends who bully that you're not going to join in. If you bully out of anger or because it's an **impulse** you can't seem to control, a counselor can help you manage your feelings. You can make healthier decisions when faced with situations in which you might have bullied in the past.

If you were bullying because you felt bad about yourself, boost your self-esteem. Write down your good qualities and strengths. Build more positive relationships with others. Your trusted adult can help you think of more ways to raise your self-esteem.

IN THE ZONE

Studies have found that helping students deal with their feelings in positive ways can reduce bullying.

Bullies who also have been victims of bullying are especially in need of rebuilding their self-esteem. They're used to acting aggressively because they've been hurt too.

19

BUILDING A BULLY-FREE SPACE

If you've bullied people in the past and know it was a mistake, you're the perfect person to take part in anti-bullying programs. You understand why it was important to change and how to move forward to help others. Taking part may also show others that you've changed.

Anti-bullying programs have been proven to reduce the amount of bullying in schools. However, not all programs are successful. People have discovered that continuing programs directed at the causes of bullying work well. Students should be taught to think before they act and learn how to have empathy for others as well.

IN THE ZONE

Every U.S. state requires its schools to talk about bullying and provides money for anti-bullying programs to be put in place.

If your school doesn't have an anti-bullying program that works, you can ask a teacher or parent to help you start one!

ANTI-BULLYING ADVOCATE

You don't have to like everyone, but it's up to you to choose not to hurt others with your words and actions. This is an important agreement that we all can make right now.

By becoming an **advocate** for those who are bullied, you can improve your school and the other communities you're a part of. You might save someone from getting hurt and probably make new friends.

Be proud to be an anti-bullying advocate. You can't change the past, but you can be kinder in the future—and make a positive difference in people's lives!

GLOSSARY

advocate: One who supports or speaks in favor of something or someone.

aggressive: Showing a readiness to attack or do harm.

counselor: Someone who talks with people about their feelings and who gives advice.

embarrassing: Causing somebody to be ashamed or ill at ease.

impulse: A sudden strong desire to do something.

reputation: The views that are held about someone.

rumor: A story passed from person to person that has not been proven to be true.

self-esteem: A feeling of having respect for yourself.

social network: A website or other application that lets users communicate by posting comments, messages, and images.

taunt: To insult someone to make them angry.

threaten: To say that you will harm someone, often to get what you want.

INDEX

WEBSITES

Due to the changing nature of Internet links, PowerKids Press has developed an online list of websites related to the subject of this book. This site is updated regularly. Please use this link to access the list: www.powerkidslinks.com/bullyfree/bully